D1709418

DO YOU REALLY WANT TO VISIT SATURN?

BY BRIDGET HEOS

ILLUSTRATED BY DANIELE FABBRI

Amicus Illustrated is published by Amicus
P.O. Box 1329, Mankato, MN 56002
www.amicuspublishing.us

Library of Congress Cataloging-in-Publication Data
Heos, Bridget.
Do you really want to visit Saturn? / by Bridget Heos;
illustrated by Daniele Fabbri. — 1st ed.
p. cm. — (Do you really want to visit—?)
Audience: K-3.
Summary: "A child astronaut takes an imaginary trip
to Saturn, learns about the harsh conditions on the gas
planet, and decides that Earth is a good home after
all. Includes solar system diagram, Saturn vs. Earth fact
chart, and glossary"—Provided by publisher.
Includes bibliographical references.
ISBN 978-1-60753-200-2 (library binding) — ISBN
978-1-60753-406-8 (ebook)
1. Saturn (Planet)—Juvenile literature. 2. Saturn
(Planet)—Exploration—Juvenile literature. I. Fabbri,
Daniele, 1978– ill. II. Title. III. Series: Do you really
want to visit—?
QB671.H46 2014
523.46—dc23
                                        2012026003

Editor: Rebecca Glaser
Designer: The Design Lab

Printed in the United States of America at
Corporate Graphics in North Mankato, Minnesota.

Date 2/2014   PO 1198

9 8 7 6 5 4 3

So you say you want to live on another planet. You really, really want to go to Saturn. But do you *really* want to go to Saturn?

DO YOU REALLY WANT TO VISIT SATURN?

Saturn is hundreds of millions of miles away. It will take you about seven years to get there. Be warned! Saturn is a dangerous place. Be sure to pack the world's best space suit, gas mask, and spaceship.

Don't pack a bike. Or a scooter. Or a skateboard. Saturn's rings may look like a racetrack from far away.

5

But when you get there, you'll see the rings are made of dust and ice chunks. Some are tiny. Many are like boulders. A few are as big as mountains. Watch out!

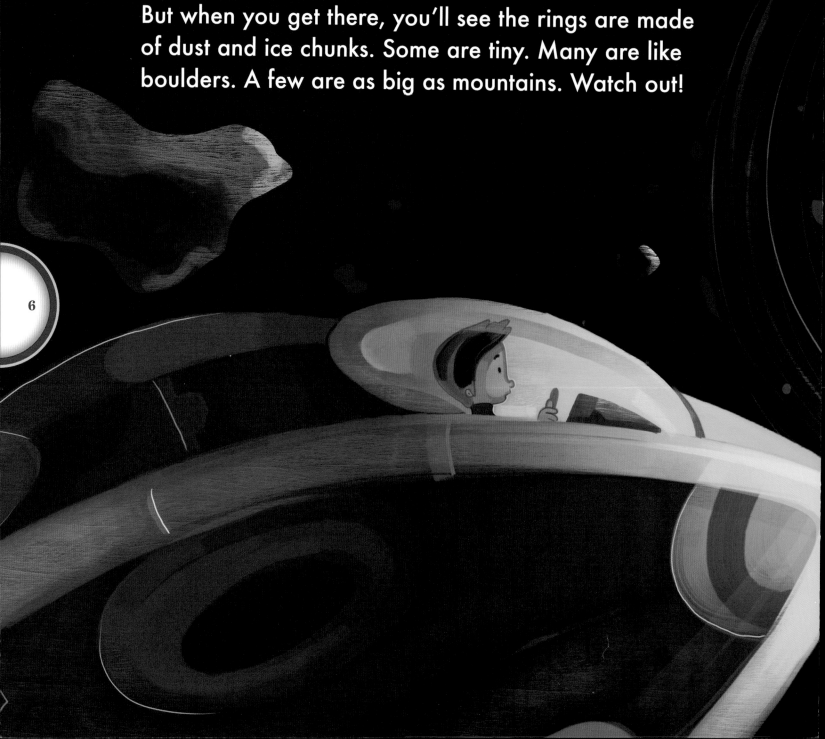

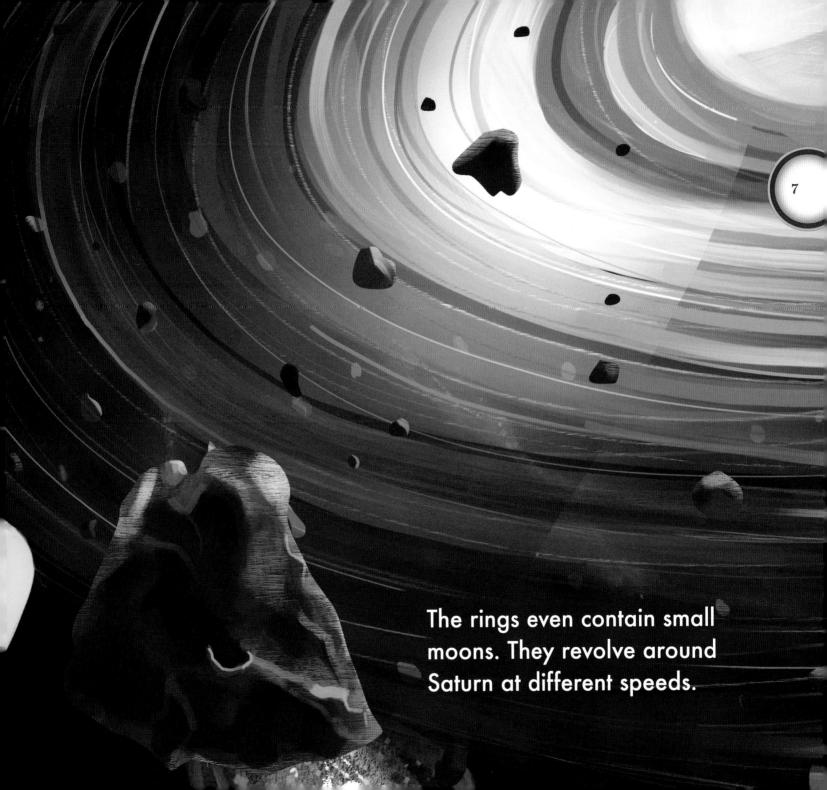

The rings even contain small moons. They revolve around Saturn at different speeds.

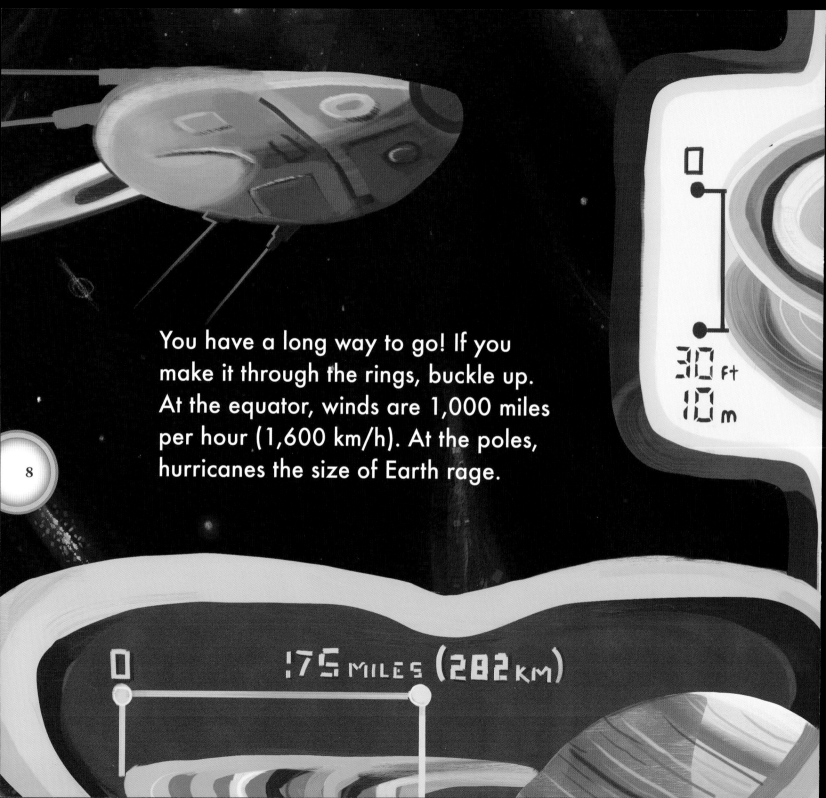

You have a long way to go! If you make it through the rings, buckle up. At the equator, winds are 1,000 miles per hour (1,600 km/h). At the poles, hurricanes the size of Earth rage.

30 ft
10 m

175 MILES (282 km)

From a distance, look at the clouds. See how they form a hexagon? Remember, don't get too close.

9

Oops!

If you make it through the icy hurricane, you'll reach thousands of miles of poisonous gas. There is no oxygen on Saturn. Instead, you'll travel through hydrogen, helium, and methane for 18,600 miles (30,000 km). Wear your gas mask!

The air will become hotter and thicker. Pressure builds.
It builds so much that helium turns to liquid and rains
down. At last, you'll reach an ocean...

...of steaming liquid hydrogen.

And that is your cue to leave. Go!

12

On your way back to Earth,
be sure to take the Moon Tour.

First you'll see the little shepherd moons: Mimas, Pan, Encke, Daphnis, Prometheus, and Pandora. They "herd" the rings, or keep them in place. Beyond the rings, visit the moon Titan!

15

With its lakes and land, Titan may remind you of Earth. Only it's orange because of the thick atmosphere. It has no oxygen, and the lakes are liquid methane. Even a space probe couldn't survive for more than a few hours.

The moon Enceladus is so cold the volcanoes spew frozen lava. You'll see a bunch of other moons, too. It's a long tour. Saturn has 61 moons in all. But the view of the planet and its rings is worth it. Too bad they're not really a racetrack.

What's the matter?
Oh, I see. You must miss Earth.
You probably miss riding
your bike, too.

There. That's better.
Home sweet block.

19

Saturn may be a challenging place to visit, but you really, really wouldn't want to live there. It's nice to look at, though.

SUN

MERCURY

VENUS

EARTH

MARS

JUPITER

SATURN

URANUS

NEPTUNE

21

How Do We Know About Saturn?

We can't actually travel to Saturn. So how do we know about the planet? Unmanned space probes have been sent to the planet to take photos and measurements. They include *Pioneer 11* (1979), *Voyagers 1* (1980) and 2 (1981), and *Cassini-Huygens* (2004). They all radioed photos and data back to Earth for scientists to study.

Earth vs. Saturn

	Earth	Saturn
Position in solar system	Third from Sun	Sixth from Sun
Average distance from Sun	93 million miles (150 million km)	886 million miles (1,427 million km)
Year (time to orbit Sun)	365 days	29.4 Earth years
Day (sunrise to sunrise)	24 hours	10 hours, 39 minutes
Diameter	7,926 miles (12,756 km)	74,900 miles (120,536 km)
Mass	1	95.16 times Earth
Air	Oxygen and nitrogen	Hydrogen, helium, methane, ammonium
Water	About 70% covered with water	Contains water ice in its rings and clouds. Its moon Enceladus may have a water ocean beneath its surface.
Moons	1	61 known moons
Places to ride your bike	Earth has lots of bike trails. Or you can ride around the block!	Saturn's rings look like a race track but are actually chunks of rocks and ice.

Glossary

atmosphere The mixture of gases that surrounds a planet or moon.

gas The form of a substance in which it expands to fill a given area.

helium A light colorless gas that does not burn. It is often used to fill balloons.

hydrogen A colorless gas that is lighter than air and catches fire easily. It can also be used to fill balloons, but it's not recommended.

lava The hot, liquid rock of a volcano.

liquid The form of a substance in which it flows freely but, unlike a gas, does not expand freely.

moon A body that circles around a planet.

oxygen A colorless gas that humans and animals need to breathe and is essential to life.

planet A large body that revolves around a sun.

pressure The weight of air or water pressing down on something.

rings The bands of dust, ice, or rocks that revolve around some planets.

volcano A vent on the surface of a planet or moon through which underground lava flows.

Read More

Aguilar, David A. *11 Planets: A New View of the Solar System*. National Geographic, 2008.

Carson, Mary Kay. *Far-out Guide to Saturn*. Enslow Publishers, 2011.

Mist, Rosalind. *Jupiter and Saturn*. QEB Publishing, 2009.

Owens, L.L. *Saturn*. Child's World, 2011.

Waxman, Laura Hamilton. *Saturn*. Lerner Publications, 2010.

Websites

Cassini Solstice Mission
http://saturn.jpl.nasa.gov/index.cfm
Learn about the Cassini Solstice Mission as it happens. The Cassini orbiter is gathering data about Saturn and its moons.

NASA Kids' Club
http://www.nasa.gov/audience/forkids/kidsclub/flash/
NASA Kids' Club features games, pictures, and information about astronauts and space travel.

StarChild: A Learning Center for Young Astronomers
http://starchild.gsfc.nasa.gov/docs/StarChild/
Click on Solar System to read facts about all the planets.

Welcome to the Planets: Saturn
http://pds.jpl.nasa.gov/planets/choices/saturn1.htm
View slideshows of the best photographs taken of Saturn, plus hear captions read aloud.

About the Author

Bridget Heos is the author of more than 40 books for children and teens, including *What to Expect When You're Expecting Larvae* (2011, Lerner). She lives in Kansas City with husband Justin, sons Johnny, Richie, and J.J., plus a dog, cat, and Guinea pig. You can visit her online at www.authorbridgetheos.com.

About the Illustrator

Daniele Fabbri was born in Ravenna, Italy, in 1978. He graduated from Istituto Europeo di Design in Milan, Italy, and started his career as a cartoon animator, storyboarder, and background designer for animated series. He has worked as a freelance illustrator since 2003, collaborating with international publishers and advertising agencies.